Busy Bears
BIG
Word Book

Busy Bear's **BIG** Word Book

In Our House

First Comes Spring

Anne Rockwell

DEAN

In Our House and *First Comes Spring* first published in Great Britain 1986
This edition first published 1993 by Dean
in association with Heinemann Young Books
a division of Reed Consumer Books Ltd
Michelin House, 81 Fulham Road, London SW3 6RB
and Auckland, Melbourne, Singapore and Toronto

Copyright © Anne Rockwell 1985

ISBN 0 603 55098 3

Produced by Mandarin Offset
Printed in China

A catalogue record of this book is available
in the British Library

In Our House

This is my family —
my mother, my father
and me.

This is the house
where we live.

This is our living room.
It is full of nice things.

What do we do in our living room?

feed
the
goldfish

dust
the
furniture

talk on the telephone

water the plant

vacuum
the
rug

play
the
cello

watch TV

play draughts

knit
warm sweaters

roast chestnuts

read books

put records
on the record player

set
the
time

dance

open
presents

change
the
light
bulb

pay bills

pull
the
curtains

milk
cocoa
bananas
potatoes

This is our kitchen.
It is full of nice things.

What do we do in our kitchen?

mop the floor

have breakfast

make lemonade

make ice cubes

throw away the rubbish

read the newspaper

drink coffee

put away the groceries

set the table

cook supper

roll out pastry

dry dishes

clean cupboards

fold the tablecloth

pack a picnic lunch

wash dishes

cut onions

make greetings cards

write the grocery list

snip parsley

beat eggs

look up recipes

polish pots and pans

This is our basement.
It is full of nice things.

What do we do in our basement?

paint
pictures

wash the clothes

fold the laundry

tie up
old newspapers

store marmalade and jam

read
the
meters

change the
fuses

check
the boiler

play ping-pong

sweep
the
floor

iron
the
clothes

This is our garage.
It is full of nice things.

What do we do in our garage?

put the car away

mend the lawnmower

plant seeds in pots

mend the hose

make a nesting box

paint the garden furniture

look for screws and nails

saw
wood

clean paintbrushes

hammer
nails

put
away
buckets
and
spades

pump up the bicycle tyres

measure
things

wax
the car

put
away
the
watering
can

This is our bathroom.
It is full of nice things.

What do we do in the bathroom?

put
dirty
clothes
in the
bin

gargle away
sore throats

clean
cuts

put on plasters

weigh
ourselves

have
a
bath

shave whiskers

sail boats

scrub
the bath

fix the plumbing

go to the toilet

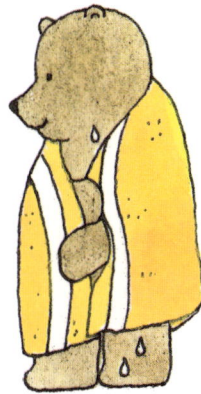
dry
ourselves

wash hands

put on perfume

shampoo
hair

brush teeth

sing in
the shower

This is my very own room.
It is full of nice things.

What do I do in my room?

get dressed

play with my teddy bear

play with my cars and trucks

build with bricks

make music

find lost toys

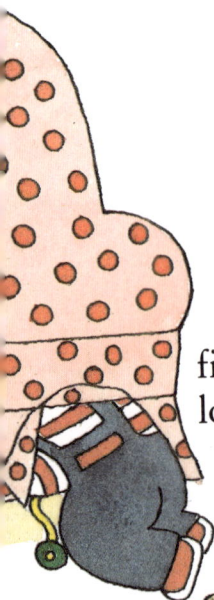

ride the rocking horse

make my bed

play puppets
with my friend

put away
my toys

colour my
colouring books

do jig-saw puzzles

put on
pyjamas

listen to
a story

put away
my shoes

count the stars

go
to
sleep

We love our house.
It is our home.

First Comes Spring

Wake up, Bear.

Look out of your window.

The daffodils and tulips are up.
The apple tree has blossoms.

This is what Bear wears today—
boots, dungarees, a check shirt
and an anorak.

For spring has come to town.
Everyone is busy.

What are they doing?

They are working and playing.

swinging

putting up
a nesting box

putting away
winter clothes

colouring
Easter Eggs

riding bicycles

skipping

having
carnivals

making mud pies

fertilizing
the lawn

watching
the birds
come back

flying
kites

cleaning windows

pruning the rosebushes

going fishing

taking away
the double
glazing

finding
wild flowers
in the woods

planting seeds

checking
the car

taking
pictures
of
spring
blossoms

finding Easter Eggs

playing
on the seesaw

painting
pictures

putting
houseplants
outside

ploughing fields

The grass in the garden is green.
The apple tree has little green apples.

Now this is what Bear wears—
trainers, shorts and a T-shirt.

For summer has come to town.
Everyone is busy.

What are they doing?

They are working
and playing.

watching ants

swimming

buying
ice-cream

reading in a hammock

weeding
the
garden

mowing
the lawn

blowing
soap bubbles

watering the rosebushes

painting
the
house

drinking
lemonade

washing the car

drying clothes
in the sun

cooking
outdoors

having picnics

playing in
the paddling pool

putting up
the tent

playing
rounders

sailing

building
a new house

The apples are red.
Orange and yellow leaves fall to the ground.

Now this is what Bear wears—
new shoes, corduroy trousers, a sweater
and a school bag.

For autumn has come to town.
Everyone is busy.

What are they doing?

They are working
and playing.

picking
apples

watching
the birds
fly
south

canoeing

going
to school

raking
leaves

building
towers with bricks

gathering
nuts

playing football

feeding
the birds

dressing up
for Hallowe'en

carving
a Jack-o'-lantern

moving into
a
new house

picking
pumpkins

chopping
wood

cutting
down
the flower stalks

putting up
double
glazing

making apple pie

putting
the houseplants
indoors

buying
new clothes

servicing
the car

The trees have lost their leaves.
Snowflakes cover the ground.

Now this is what Bear wears—
rubber boots, a snowsuit, a scarf,
a hat and warm mittens.

For winter has come to town.
Everyone is busy.

What are they doing?

They are working and playing.

ice-skating

visiting
Father Christmas

tobogganing

having colds

buying
presents

lighting
candles

making
angels

singing carols

drinking cocoa

clearing the snow

wrapping presents

putting
a
holly
wreath
on
the door

putting
food
out for
the birds

bringing
a Christmas tree
home

clearing
the path

throwing
snowballs

building
an igloo

skiing

putting
lights
on
the
Christmas
tree

baking biscuits

The Bear Family sits
by the nice, warm fire.

What will happen when winter
is over?

Spring will come again.